Carluke

in old picture postcards

by
Margaret J.C. Logan and Christine H. Warren
of Carluke Parish Historical Society

Second edition

European Library - Zaltbommel/Netherlands MCMLXXXVIII

GB   ISBN 90 288 3421 4 / CIP

© 1986 European Library - Zaltbommel/Netherlands

European Library in Zaltbommel/Netherlands publishes among other things the following series:

IN OLD PICTURE POSTCARDS *is a series of books which sets out to show what a particular place looked like and what life was like in Victorian and Edwardian times. A book about virtually every town in the United Kingdom is to be published in this series. By the end of this year about 300 different volumes will have appeared. 1,500 books have already been published devoted to the Netherlands with the title* **In oude ansichten.** *In Germany, Austria and Switzerland 650, 100 and 25 books have been published as* **In alten Ansichten;** *in France by the name* **En cartes postales anciennes** *and in Belgium as* **In oude prentkaarten** *and/or* **En cartes postales anciennes** *150 respectively 400 volumes have been published.*

For further particulars about published or forthcoming books, apply to your bookseller or direct to the publisher.

INTRODUCTION

The Parish of Carluke lies in the north of the district of Clydesdale in Strathclyde region and stretches from the floor of the Clyde Valley up the steep river banks to a plateau about 1,000 feet above sea level.

Many people have tried to discover the origins of the name 'Carluke', but with little success. Long before the Reformation in 1560, possibly as early as the 14th century, the monks of Kelso left their ancient church and lands in the Forest of Mauldslie, on the banks of the Clyde, and built a new church, where the town's old graveyard now lies. The church was for long known as Forest Kirk, but in documents going back as far as the 12th century it was called 'Eglismalesock'. Various spellings of this have been found but it is generally agreed that 'Eglis' means church and that 'malesock' refers to a Saint's name. There seems to be no proof that the church was ever dedicated to St. Luke, but for some reason the old Carluke church was named as St. Luke's in the first Ordnance Survey map. The first part of the name 'Carluke' is probably derived from the Gaelic 'carn' meaning a cairn or a high place, which is certainly appropriate, but the origins of the second part of the name remain a mystery.

When the monks of Kelso moved to their new church they were given lands in the vicinity, in exchange for those which they had owned in the Forest of Mauldslie. These lands became known as the lands of Kirkton and Kirkstyle, and it was the village of Kirkstyle, close by the church, which in time developed into the town of Carluke. In 1662, Kirkstyle became a Burgh of Barony united with the Barony of Kirkton, when Charles II granted a charter to Captain Walter Lockhart and his wife. This charter gave Captain Lockhart and his heirs many powers, including the right to have a market cross, to hold fairs twice a year, to erect a courthouse and to appoint court officials. However, the village of Kirkstyle consisted only of a few cottages at that time and little effort seems to have been made to expand the population. By 1695, in the poll tax list, the village seems to have become officially known as Carluke, but even then, only six families lived there.

In many ways it is surprising that Carluke survived to become a town at all. Even in the 1770s, according to the First Statistical Account, there were only four or five houses in the village. However, by the end of the century, there were several shops and a population of about 380. At that time, new streets were added to expand the village, such as North and South Street (later called Rankin and Cassells Street), Clyde Street, Market Place and Chapel Street and thus were laid the foundations of the town we know today. There must have been many reasons for this rapid expansion of Carluke, such as improvements in roads, improved farming methods and the benefits of industrialisation in the surrounding area. A thriving weaving industry developed in Carluke at the beginning of the nineteenth century, when many inhabitants were hand-loom weavers or hoziers.

From then on, Carluke steadily expanded, despite the decline of the weaving industry. The building of the Stirling to Carlisle turnpike road through Carluke in 1823, the commencement of the mining of the rich mineral resources in the parish and the building of the railway ensured that Carluke would become a prosperous town.

By the middle of the last century there were shops and trades of all descriptions and Carluke had become a centre of commerce for the surrounding area. According to the Ordnance Gazetteer of 1892, Carluke was clearly a prosperous town with banks, agricultural and horticultural societies, a Useful Knowledge Society with library and a museum. There were also five hotels and inns, where visitors to the town could stay; Carluke has always been in a picturesque rural area with strong farming and fruit growing traditions and the town clearly remained attractive despite the extensive mining around the town.

Carluke's prosperity continued right into the 20th century. Older residents of the town can paint a fascinating picture of life at this time. The shops opened until 10 p.m. on a Saturday and the pavements were crowded to overflowing with people from all over the parish who had walked there after work. Many remember with enthusiasm how local people took a keen interest in the affairs of the town which they themselves, through the Parish Council and School Board, helped to run. Pride of place in their memories must go to the Rankin Memorial Town Hall, scene of active (sometimes acrimonious!) political debates, dances, plays, operas and countless other important events.

Slowly the character of the town began to change. The introduction of radio and improvements in transport ensured that people would never again be so totally involved in the life of the town. One by one, the pits closed and unemployment began to rise. People had to look outwith the town for work and many of the traditional family names began to disappear from above the shops.

Over the last twenty years, Carluke has assumed a new role as a dormitory town, chosen for its proximity to industrial Lanarkshire and Glasgow. The population has steadily increased until Carluke is now the largest town in Clydesdale District with over 12,000 inhabitants.

Once again, Carluke is becoming a thriving town, its name known to many all over the world as the home of Scott's jam. The town centre has become a modern pedestrian precinct and the wide variety of sporting and leisure facilities ensures that Carluke people lead very busy lives!

We would like to thank the many friends and members of Carluke Parish Historical Society who have helped with the compilation of these photographs, particularly our honorary president, Dr. Daniel Martin, whose support and guidance we value so highly.

1. This is Carluke Cross around 1906. The main Carlisle to Stirling road, which runs through the centre of the picture, was built as a turnpike road in 1823. The square building on the right, originally the City of Glasgow Bank, later became the National Bank, then the National Commercial Bank. It is now the Royal Bank of Scotland. On the corner below the conical tower was the Douglas Bar. The name has now changed to The County Bar.

Market Place, Carluke   Valentines Series   36203

2. The rough ground in the picture was the Market Place of the town where fairs were held in March, May, July and October. 'The market' was transformed by the local council in the 1930s. Formal gardens and tarmac paths now make 'the market' a favourite meeting place for townspeople in the summer months. On Christmas Eve, 'the market' is filled with thousands of young and old carol singers awaiting the annual visit of Santa Claus, who arrives on a horse-driven cart and distributes an orange to each child before attending to his main work of the evening! The Crown Hotel at the foot of 'the market' is still standing. The thatched cottages on the right were replaced by the Masonic Lodge and Hall, a gift to the Order of Freemasons by Lord Newlands of Mauldslie.

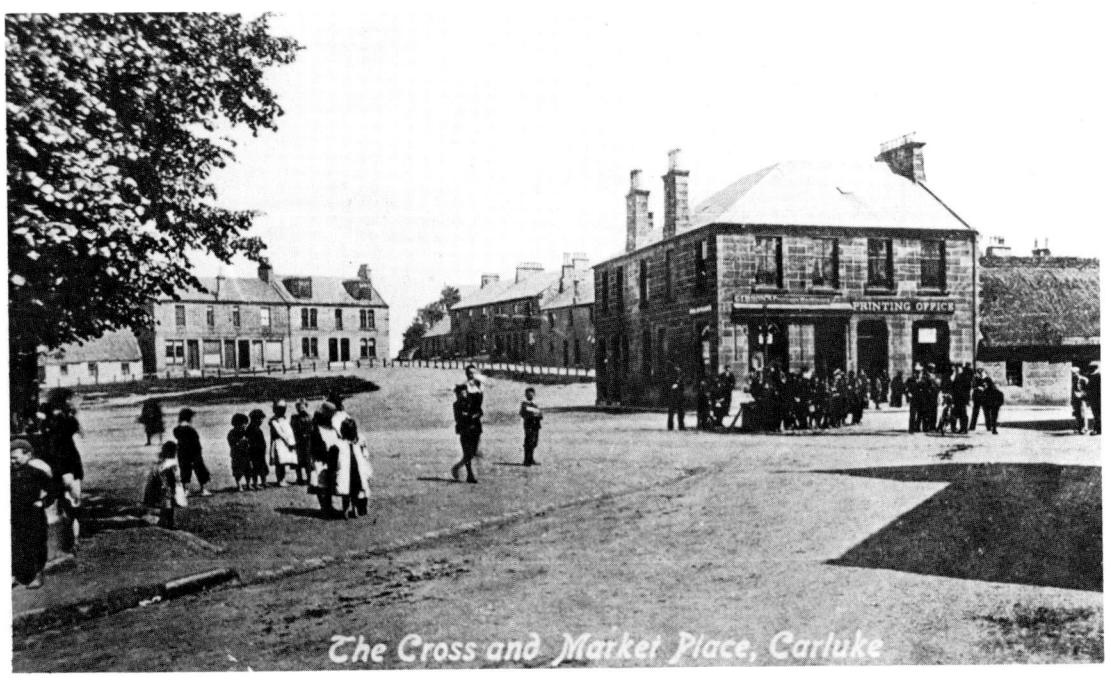

The Cross and Market Place, Carluke

3. This view of 'the market' includes the Printing Office of the local weekly paper, the Carluke Gazette, founded by Andrew Beveridge in 1906. The paper was sold to Jacob Bell just after the First World War and remained in the hands of the Bell family until 1972, when it was taken over by Johnston (Falkirk) Ltd. The thatched building is The Wee Thackit Inn which lost its thatch in the 1950s in a fire. The men in the centre are standing round a lamp-post which was the traditional meeting place each Hogmanay. Hundreds of townspeople gathered there to greet the New Year, which was heralded in by the Town Hall bell, as well as church bells, town bands and factory hooters. This custom has now died out.

4. The biggest event ever seen in the town's Market Place was the homecoming of Corporal William Angus V.C. He is pictured here supported by Lord Newlands, Lord Lieutenant of the County, and Lieutenant James Martin. Angus was awarded his Victoria Cross in June 1915. He brought Lieutenant Martin, also a Carluke man, back from no-man's-land between the trenches near Givenchy, France, and suffered forty wounds, including the loss of an eye. His commanding officer called his action 'the bravest deed ever done in the history of the British Army'.

5. A crowd of 25,000 people made their way by foot, road and rail to see the presentation to the town's first Victoria Cross winner on 4th September 1915. Angus arrived at the railway station and was transported at the head of a motor cavalcade to the Market Place, where he was presented with various awards, including £1,000 collected in the town and a gold watch and chain from the man he saved, Lieutenant Martin.

6. This photograph shows Angus with the town's second Victoria Cross winner, Sergeant Thomas Caldwell. Caldwell won his medal on 31st October 1918, ten days before the war ended, by capturing single-handedly an enemy machine gun position and taking eighteen prisoners. The machine-gunners had been holding up the British advance at Audenarde until Sergeant Caldwell performed his heroic deed. A presentation ceremony was held for Caldwell in January 1919 in the Town Hall, when he received similar awards to those made to Angus. Carluke is quite unique in its record for winning Victoria Cross medals. In the Second World War, Donald Cameron was awarded the Victoria Cross for commanding the midget submarine which mined the Tirpitz. Carluke has named a street after each of the men and also after another First World War hero, Sergeant Arthur Ramage.

MARKET ROAD, CARLUKE.

7. In the latter half of the nineteenth century, the differences of opinion between the churches in the town were many and varied. A number of enlightened people, including John Henshilwood, the grocer, and William Martin, founder of Carluke's Baptist Church, began to feel that this was wrong. They decided, whilst taking a Sunday walk together, to build a hall which would be non-denominational; thus the Evangelistic Hall was built in 1878. It can be seen in the right foreground of this picture. Tinto Terrace, the two-storey building on the left of Market Road, has now disappeared.

8. Further up Market Road stands this imposing building. This is the Drill Hall, built by public subscription for the Lanarkshire Yeomanry in 1905-06, in memory of the men who lost their lives in the Boer War. Many Carluke men served in the Lanarkshire Yeomanry, affectionately known as the 'Lan Yeo'. Its origins go back into the mists of time, but people remember it today as a regiment of the Territorials. In earlier times it was a cavalry unit and some people say there were stables for the horses at Castlehill. By the Second World War, however, it had become a tank unit. Two cannon used to stand outside the building; one of them was a naval cannon, the other was captured and brought home from the Boer War by the Yeomanry. Many of Carluke's older residents also have fond recollections of glass cases of stuffed animals, which were inside the building at the entrance. In recent years, the Drill Hall has been used by various organisations in the town, including the squash club and the boxing club.

9. This photograph shows the town's High Street around 1900. On the right hand side of the street can be seen the old post office. The first Carluke telephone exchange was sited in the bedroom of the house above the post office. The exchange was manned night and day by two sisters, Mrs. Somerville and Miss Jackson. Next door was the painter's shop of Alex Harvie. His youngest son, Sergeant William Harvie of the Royal Scots Greys, was the first Carluke man to die on active service in the First World War. The building with the twin urns was the Parish Council Chambers and now houses the local office of the registrar of Births, Deaths and Marriages. On the other side of the street can be spotted the old chemist shop sign of mortar and pestle. This was Hinksman's shop, from which many people bought Hinksman's Asthma Reliever, once reknowned throughout the country.

10. Originally the Post Office was part of Aikman's stationery shop which was just down from Hinksman's chemist's shop. This photograph shows the Carluke Post Office in 1906 and it may well be that the photograph was taken to mark the occasion when the Post Office moved across to the site shown in the previous picture. The postmistress at this time was Miss Aikman and many of the other staff have been identified including Adam Watson, a local poet (front row, far left). The Post Office is no longer in the High Street, having moved to larger premises in Kirkton Street in 1960.

11. Mis Peggy Burton's shop in the High Street shows a typical fancy goods and toy shop with an infinite variety of goods for sale. The boys in the photograph are her nephews, Archie and Thomas Horsburgh. This photograph was taken around 1912 and clearly shows clothing and footwear worn by boys at this time.

12. Carluke Parish Council had its own fire engine and firemen as shown in this photograph, thought to be taken behind the Town Chambers. Little is known about this group of men, but the fire brigade disappeared from the town and was replaced by a single firefighter who had a barrow to tackle fires.

13. This is the bottom of the High Street around 1900. The little boy in the foreground on the right is standing outside Spence and Young's, the newsagent's. The shop next door belonged to Thomas Gray, a well-known baker, who won many medals for his tasty oatcakes. Next door, standing back from the street, is the Black Bull Inn, one of the oldest buildings in the town. It dates back to the 1790s and was once used as a meeting place for many town organisations. In December 1859, a large gathering met to discuss the threatened invasion of Napoleon III and a volunteer force of sixty men was raised to defend the Parish. The public house has retained its name to the present day. The bank building which we pointed out in the first picture can be clearly seen at the top of the High Street.

14. Chapel Street shows Johnny Morton's grocery shop on the corner. Here the staff would weigh and wrap in brown bags items such as flour, tea, sugar. Tobacco would be sliced and wrapped into ¼oz., ½oz. etc. Cheeses were delivered whole, wrapped in sacking, and cut with thin wire. Butter would be delivered in barrels and patted into the required weights. Morton's sold their own blend of tea, 'Ensign Tea', which was sold in white packets with a red cross on the front.

15. Further up Chapel Street can be seen the church now known as Kirkstyle Baptist Church. Built in 1880 by the Congregation of the United Original Secession Church, it replaced the Seceders' Meeting House, built on an adjacent site in 1801. When the new church was erected, a house for the beadle (part of which is shown in the photograph) was built on the site of the meeting house.

16. The High Mill stands at the top of Chapel Street, which used to be called Windmill Brae. The mill tower was built about 1797 by David Dick, on land he leased from the local laird, Captain Charles Hamilton of Kirkton and Fairholm. The mill must have been successful, as it was mentioned in an advertisement of 1817 which extolled the virtues of Carluke in the hope of attracting people to the town. Certainly, David Dick became a man of some standing in the town, as he was appointed Baron Baillie in 1815. For some reason, however, plans to build a courthouse in the town did not come to fruition. Some years later, David Dick handed over the running of the mill to two of his sons, James, a millwright and engineer, and William, a miller. They converted the mill to steam power and added several structures to the original tower, including a threshing mill. The family tradition of milling continued right into the early 20th century. However, the mill fell into disuse about 1930, having been converted to suction gas power by James Dick only 15 years earlier.

17. Carnwath Road, formerly Crawforddyke Street, is an extension of the High Street heading towards Carnwath. The Rankin Memorial Hall stands on the right and the Evangelical Union Church is pictured on the left foreground. This church was built in 1853 on the site of the Sparrow Inn. Of the buildings in this picture, only the church remains.

18. This is an earlier photograph of the Rankin Memorial Hall and Library built in 1884 by public subscription, in memory of Dr. Daniel Reid Rankin. The site for the hall and £1,000 was given by James Brownlee of the City Sawmills in Glasgow on condition that the townspeople raised the rest. Mr. Brownlee was a native of Carluke. The clock tower was later extended so that it could be seen from all over the town (see previous picture). The row of thatched cottages was later replaced by a two-storey building known as Bow's Buildings, after the bakery business on the premises. These buildings were demolished in 1979.

19. Doctor Daniel Rankin was born in Carluke in 1805. He began a career in law but changed to medicine and studied at the Faculty of Physicians and Surgeons in Glasgow. He chose to practice in Carluke despite other opportunities and became a well-loved and much respected figure in the town. He never charged the poorer townspeople, who knew he could be relied upon for help and advice, no matter what the problem. Rankin gave lectures to advance scientific knowledge, studied local geology and contributed greatly to Scottish geological knowledge. Indeed, Louis Agassiz, the reknowned French geologist, named a fossil after him. Doctor Rankin alwo wrote 'Notices Historical, Statistical and Biographical, relating to the Parish of Carluke from 1288 to 1874'. This carefully researched book is much valued today as a source of information on Carluke's past. Daniel Rankin died in 1882.

20. This bell-tower was built in 1715 and stands in Carluke's oldest graveyard. It was erected next to the old Carluke Kirk which was built at an unknown date when Forest Kirk, an early religious settlement on the Mauldslie Estate on the banks of the Clyde, was abandoned. According to Blind Harry, William Wallace was chosen to be Warden of Scotland at Forest Kirk in 1297. A plaque on the bell-tower thanks James Ross and his uncles, Thomas and James Gibb of Quebec, for donating money to the town to extend and wall the graveyard. James Ross became a multi-millionaire after leaving Carluke when he was 15 years old.

21. The Parish Church, now St. Andrew's Church, was built in 1799 to replace the old Carluke Kirk. It stands at the top of Mount Stewart Street and in those days was called the 'Visible Kirk', because it could be seen from Glasgow Green. The design, by Henry Bell, of the steamship Comet fame, cost 2½ guineas. Shortly after it opened, the original slim spire was struck by lightning. In 1820, the spire was replaced by the present tower. The porches were added in 1890 by Alexander Tudhope.

22. Hamilton Street is pictured here around 1905. The public water pump at the corner of the High Street has disappeared but the buildings on the right remain the same today. William Brownlee, the draper, had the shop on the corner and lived in the house above. This house later became the Holyoake Tearooms of Carluke Co-operative Society which eventually owned the whole building. The tearooms were a popular venue for functions such as wedding receptions, parties and club meetings.

23. Just down from Brownlee's, on the corner of Cassells Street, was Henshilwood's. The figure in the doorway is Robert Forrest, aged about 16. Mr. Forrest now owns a large nursery and tearoom at Braidwood. The picture was taken around 1930.

24. Further down Hamilton Street, the carts are standing outside the town smiddy while the horses are waiting to be shod. This smiddy is still in operation today. The boot factory, which was directly opposite the smiddy, was burned down around 1925. Also in the photograph is St. John's Church. This was the Free Church set up after the disruption within the Church of Scotland in 1843. The present building was erected around 1864 and can seat 650.

25. This postcard of the Old Bridge End, around 1900, shows the original road from Carlisle to Stirling. According to Dr. Rankin, a band of stragglers of Bonnie Prince Charlie's army passed along this road on their retreat from Derby in 1746. They stopped in Carluke long enough to help themselves to food and horses before leaving the town.

26. This is Kirkton Street around 1930. The Caledonian Arms and the Railway Inn stand on the right. On the left can be seen the petrol pumps outside the old bus garage. The lorry is thought to belong to Stewart the joiner, who had, and still has, premises in Union Street. The lorry is a Clyde.

27. The Laigh, or Low, Mill in Carluke was a watermill, which stood on the Minister's Burn near to Stark's Bridge on the present Lanark Road. It was used until 1940 and, during the Second World War, ground peanuts for oil. Stark's Bridge was thus called because the Burnside Sawmill, started by Mr. Andrew Stark, stood on the other side of the bridge from the Laigh Mill.

28. In 1832, some members of the Established Church seceded and formed a new congregation which found temporary accommodation in the Laigh Mill. A church to house this congregation was erected in 1833 at a cost of £822, on land feued from the Laird of Kirkton and Fairholm. The foundation stone of this United Presbyterian Church contains small bottles of wine and oil, copies of newspapers of the time, one of each of the current coins of the realm and a document recording the origin of the congregation. The designation Kirkton was adopted in 1900 when the Free Church and United Presbyterian Church united.

29. The milk cart with its churns was a common sight around the town. This is the Whiteshaw Dairy Cart in Station Road. Mr. James Barr owned Whiteshaw Farm and the dairy herd, but he rented out the cows to 'bouars'. These bouars milked the herd and ran the dairy, selling milk, butter and cheese to the townspeople. The milk carts came round the town twice daily after the milking. Customers would take their own jugs out to the cart and the milkman would fill them from a tap on the churn, using a tin pint measure.

30. Kirkton House, reputed to have been the oldest inhabited house in Lanarkshire, was demolished about 1962. An old stone used in one of the many additions to the house was dated 1600. King Charles II stayed here on one occasion, a story given more credibility because the ground to the east of the house is recorded as 'roialdikes' (Royal Dykes) in the 1695 Poll Tax List. Major Weir, the infamous wizard, who was burned at the stake for sorcery, was born here in 1599. His ghost is said to have haunted Kirkton House.

Wellgreen, Carluke

31. This is the Wellgreen in Carluke. Like most towns, Carluke had numerous wells dotted around the town before it had a piped water supply. Occasionally a well is uncovered but usually it is filled in for reasons of safety. However, this public well was rescued and rebuilt in the 1960s. Behind the Wellgreen is the primary school known as the 'Wee' School. This was built by the heritors of the parish to replace the old school at Carluke Cross because the new turnpike road was considered to be too dangerous for the children! The 'Wee' School was opened in 1841 and was later extended on several occasions as the school population increased. It was demolished about 1980, and a new primary called Kirkton Primary took its place.

Market Place School, Carluke. *The Happy days of yore*

32. When pupils were ready to leave the 'Wee' School, at the age of eight, they naturally went to the 'Big' School, or Carluke Higher Grade as it became. There they stayed until they were 14, hoping to gain the Intermediate Certificate. The building was erected in 1876 and stands in Market Road near to the High Mill. There were no facilities for physical education until 1907, when a hall was added to the 'Wee' School. After that, boys and girls were marched at separate times down to the hall for periods of physical training. The emphasis on physical training came about as a result of the Boer War when the government was horrified at the poor physical condition of army volunteers. The tower on the building housed the school bell which was used until electric bells were introduced around 1960. The bell was recently rediscovered and nows stands fully restored in the new High School in Carnwath Road.

33. The staff of Carluke School in 1927 have all been identified. They are, back row: Wm. Marr, Jas. Young, Hy Fielding, and Hunter. Second back: A. Lightbody, the janitor, E. Cargil, A. Wilson, M. Wallace, C. Davidson, I. Russell, H. Russell and Sgt. Morton. Middle: J. Hastie, H. Bradford, J.R. Angus, J. Hamilton, A. Walker and F. Irvine. Second front: A. Anderson, J. Laughland, J. Weir, M. Cassels, McLean, A. Gibson, E. Frame and S. Phillips. Front: J. Paterson, W. Skeoch, N. Allison, J. Fordyce, J. Gass and H.P. Thornton.

34. The School Board was elected every three years by public election. It had the power to raise finance on the local rates for educational provision in the parish. The men seated here are having a board meeting in the hall of the 'Wee' School. They are from the left, clockwise: J. Paterson, J. McKay, W. Hamilton, Dr. Barr, T. Grossart, E.N. Ferguson, A. Birrell and J. McMahon. The man standing on the left is Jacob Bell, owner of the Carluke Gazette. On the right is Mr. Shirkey, a reporter. The business was reported verbatim and awaited by the townspeople with great expectation!

35. On 9th July 1914 King George V and Queen Mary visited Mauldslie Castle as luncheon guests of Lord and Lady Newlands. Lord Newlands was James Hozier who married Lady Mary Cecil in 1880. The Hozier family had acquired Mauldslie in 1850. The Royal visit was a great occasion in the parish; schools were closed and flag-waving children were marched down to line the estate roads. The guard-of-honour was made up of the Lanarkshire Yeomanry who marched the two miles from Carluke to take up position.

36. Mauldslie Castle was erected in 1792-93 by Thomas, 5th Earl of Hyndford, from a design by Adam of Edinburgh. The last wing was completed in 1890 and yet only 45 years later this impressive building was demolished. The second Lord Newlands died without issue and the castle was inherited by a nephew who unfortunately was unable to maintain it. On Friday 3rd November, 1933 at 2 p.m. every building and piece of land on the estate was auctioned off by J. & J. Marshall, the Carluke auctioneers. The castle was demolished, although one tower was transported stone by stone and re-erected at Hill of Kilncadzow Farm by Mr. T. Blackwood.

37. The Mauldslie Lodge and Gatehouse shown here lead to a bridge over the River Clyde. The castle stood on the banks of this great river, now a favourite fishing ground for local anglers. The Lodge was recently renovated and is once more inhabited.

38. This is a picture of Rosebank village, built by Lord Newlands to house his estate workers. As it stands on the opposite bank of the river from Mauldslie Castle it is actually in the Parish of Dalserf. On the right stands the Popinjay Hotel, built in 1882. The hotel is named after the 'popping jay', an archery target. Tradition has it that the hotel is built near the site of an archery contest described in 'Old Mortality' by Sir Walter Scott. The hotel is still a popular eating place today.

39. Milton Lockhart was built in 1829 in the Scottish Baronial style by Mr. William Lockhart, M.P. for the County. He was the brother of John Gibson Lockhart, biographer and son-in-law of Sir Walter Scott. The famous author chose the site, and the library was a copy of Scott's library at Abbotsford. Now this magnificent building is a ruin, but its marvellous carved gateway, beside a three arch stone bridge over the Clyde, is a listed building.

40. The estate of Hallcraig was originally part of the Forest of Mauldslie. According to Dr. Rankin's History of Carluke, Hallcraig is mentioned in a document of 1572 which charged Alexander Weir of Hallcraig, amongst many others, of murder and treason, after the death of Darnley, husband of Mary Queen of Scots. Shortly afterwards the estate was acquired by the Hamilton family, in whose hands it remained for over one hundred and fifty years. In the 19th century large parts of the estate, including Whiteshaw and Castlehill, were sold for mining. There is a connection between Hallcraig and Carluke's most eminent son, Major General William Roy, F.R.S., 1726-1790, as both his father and grandfather were factors there. Not only did Roy pursue a distinguished career in the army but he undertook valuable work in the fields of archaeology, cartography and surveying. His maps are now housed in the British Library. Roy is acknowledged as the founder of the Ordnance Survey, although a National Survey was not actually undertaken until a year after his death. In 1783, with the encouragement and financial support of George III, he measured a baseline at Hanslow, Middlesex for all trigonometrical measurements later used in Ordnance Survey mapping. For this work he received the Copley Medal from the Royal Society in 1787.

41. St. Athanasius Church was solemnly blessed and opened on 13th September 1857 by Bishop Murdoch, Bishop of Castabala and Vicar Apostolic of the Western District of Scotland. This photograph shows the interior of the church, long before its renovations in 1984. In 1849 Father Black was placed in charge of the Upper Ward of Lanarkshire and he established a Mission in Lanark and Mass Centres in the surrounding areas. The first meeting place in Carluke was a hall at the back of the Commercial Hotel in Kirkton Street, where the Holy Sacrifice was offered monthly. In 1855, Father Black purchased a piece of ground and a two-roomed thatched cottage in Mount Stewart Street from the Coltness Iron Company. This cottage became a temporary chapel until a church could be built, and afterwards was used as a school for Catholic children under the instruction of Mr. Daniel Casey.

42. This picture was taken during the First World War and shows part of the Dyke Row in Carluke. It was a miners' row and is typical of many of the rows which were scattered all over the parish, e.g. Furnace, Heather, Engine and Thornton's. The rows housed the families of men who mined for coal, limestone and ironstone. In those days many houses did not have a piped water supply and rainwater was collected in barrels. In this photograph, gutters under the thatched roof can be seen leading to each house's water barrel.

43. Roadmeetings Hospital is on the road Kilncadzow, originally spelled 'Kilcago' and still pronounced locally as 'Kilcaiggie'. It was originally built as a sanitorium and became the local 'fever hospital' after the First Wold War. Word has it that there was a yellow fever wagon with red wheels which took the sick off to the hospital! Roadmeetings is now a geriatric hospital.

44. Many people were employed on farms in Carluke at the turn of the century. This is a group of workers at Langshaw Farm, standing in front of the byre. The women are wearing thibbit aprons, which were spun from the wool of the blackface sheep, and craizes – the long headdresses worn to protect the neck when working in the fields. Langshaw Farm, with its crow-stepped gables, is probably the oldest house in the parish and is now a listed building. However, the story handed down through generations, that Oliver Cromwell once slept there, must be taken with a large pinch of salt!

45. The type of mill shown in this photograph was known locally as 'The Big Mill'. It was a travelling mill which was introduced when farms grew to such a size that the older, smaller threshing units could not cope with the size of the crop. The mill was drawn by a huge steam traction engine which also powered the unit using a system of belts and gears. Each farmer booked the mill at a time to suit his needs. By common consent, every farmer loaned a member of his staff or family to help at the farm where the threshing was being carried out.

46. After harvesting, the sheaves were led in to the stackyard where stacks were built around a tripod of poles until it was time for the visit of the Big Mill. After the threshing, the stacks were rebuilt. Nowadays, stacks are a rarity, although the Muirs of Crawfordwalls Farm continued to use horses and the old traditional methods of farming right into the late 1970s.

47. Mr. & Mrs. William Gilchrist are standing in the yard of Oldhill Farm around 1910. Mr. Gilchrist is sitting on his 'soor milk cairt'. Soor milk was sold around the town and was used either by housewives for baking or as a refreshing drink.

48. During the First Wold War, ordinary people and organisations contributed a great deal to the War Effort, none more so than the Women's Work Party. This shows one of their many tasks – gathering sphagnum moss, which was dried and used as field bandages on the battlefields. The refuse was made into stretcher pillows.

49. Thomas Prentice had his saddler's shop in Hamilton Street, Carluke. This photograph shows the firm's stall at the Highland Show, Cupar in July 1912. The site of the show used to change each year, before the permanent showground was opened at Ingliston, near Edinburgh. Stall holders would thus send out advertising postcards, inviting would-be customers to visit their stall. Harness for riding, working and carriage horses was made and supplied by Mr. Prentice. His would have been a busy shop, for not only was Carluke in the midst of farmland, but the parish also had a famous hackney stud at Thornholm near Yieldshields. The stud was founded by William Scott of the jam-making family.

50. Strawberry picking was, and still is, a seasonal job around Carluke. The fruit was sent to preserve works in the parish. The longest running and only surviving of these works is that of R. & W. Scott in Clyde Street. Robert and William Scott came to the Orchard Estate in the 1860s. At first they sold their fruit in Carluke and Glasgow by horse and cart. In 1880 they opened Clydesdale Preserve Works and began producing jam. The firm has expanded until it now exports all over the world and occupies many of the buildings in Clyde Street near the Cross.

51. Drainage tiles for fields led to great improvements in agriculture in the nineteenth century. Carluke had a number of tile works in the parish. This is a group of workers at Gibson's Milton Tile Works around 1920.

52. 'Slaghill' No 4 Pit was at Castlehill, Carluke and was owned by The Shotts Iron Company. This picture was taken around 1900 and shows at the back: unknown; George Horsburgh; unknown; John Paul. Front: Robert Lachlan; unknown; unknown. The pit was called 'Slaghill' because it was beside a great heap of ironstone slag, left behind from the Castlehill Ironworks which operated from 1838 to 1886.

53. This is a shunting pug used at Castlehill around 1887. Johnny Walker, the driver (behind the chimney), was later killed when a pug derailed around 1912. George Horsburgh, the cashier for Shotts Iron Company, is seated centre.

54. This photograph shows the washing machines in Carluke Hand and Steam Laundry around 1904. The laundry operated from a site in Sandy Road. It was advertised as 'The Most up-to-date Laundry in the Country', having been built 'on the latest and most improved scientific plans'. Apparently, one of the reasons for choosing this particular site for the laundry was that it was on the outskirts of the town and quite free from smoke! Nowadays, Sandy Road is a built-up area and regarded as fairly central to the town. Not only the prices but also the articles sent for cleaning have greatly changed since those days. For example, ladies' woollen combinations cost 2½d. each, morning dresses cost one shilling, children's starched shirts cost 2½d. and antimacassars cost from 2d. to 6d. each. There was also a carpet beating department which charged about 1½d. per yard to hand beat heavy duty carpets. The laundry closed some years ago and the buildings area now used by a variety of small firms.

55. In 1861, nineteen Carluke men formed the Carluke Equitable Pioneer Society. These men decided to set up shop and provide goods at reasonable prices for the people of Carluke. They first rented a shop at the corner of Rankin Street and Market Road. The Society expanded quickly. Eventually it had bakery premises, butchers, fish, dairy, dressmaking, millinery, fruit, hardware, footware and chemist shops in Carluke. There were also stores in other villages in the parish. This photograph shows the Crossford Branch.

56. Crossford village has the distinction of lying in three parishes. The greatest part is in the parish of Lesmahagow, with very small portions lying in the parishes of Lanark and Carluke. The postal address, however, has always been Carluke and many people regard the River Clyde as the parish boundary. Crossford bridge was built in 1852. It stands about a hundred yards above the original ford on the old road to Lanark. The toll-house at this bridge was a very busy place, as much of the fruit from the orchards on the banks of the Clyde and the coal from the nearby mines was sent to markets, via the local railway station. This was at Braidwood and meant a long haul over the bridge and up the steep braes. The toll for pedestrians was a halfpenny and vehicles were charged on a variable scale. In the late 1870s the toll-collector took in scarce a penny when the river froze over and all his customers crossed the ice to save paying the toll!

57. The Tower and Fortalice of Braidwood, or Halbar Tower as it is known locally, stands on the steep braes between the villages of Braidwood and Crossford. No definite dating on the age of the tower is known but it is mentioned in an act of 1581. The tower is in good condition, as it was extensively renovated in 1861 by Sir Norman MacDonald-Lockhart, whose family have had possession of the tower since the end of the seventeenth century.

58. About three hundred yards away from the Tower of Halbar stands the Dales, formerly known as Daleville House. This was the home of Dr. J.R.S. Hunter, eminent geologist and antiquarian, who formed the 'Braidwood Collection', which included fossils, coins and books. It was considered at the time to be the most important collection of its kind ever amassed by a private individual and was housed in a museum which Dr. Hunter had built at the side of his house. This picture shows (on the right) Dr. Hunter-Selkirk, as he became known after his marriage to Mary Selkirk, daughter of a local mine owner, with Professor John Stuart Blackie of Edinburgh. The table at which they are seated was used for communion by the Covenanters at their field conventicles, the Bible belonged to Margaret Wilson, one of the women drowned at Wigton in 1684, and the sword belonged to Gavin Hamilton Park of Mauldslie, who was hanged and quartered in Edinburgh in 1666. The sword in Hunter-Selkirk's hand belonged to the Hunters of Melrose and was used in many Covenanting battles, including Bothwell Brig.

59. This photograph of Braidwood is taken outside the village shop on the left. Today, this part of the village is referred to as Lower Braidwood and the little shop now houses the post office. The part of the village beside Braidwood Station was originally called Harestanes. The lands of Braidwood were granted as a Burgh of Barony to John de Monfod in 1326 for his homage and service to Robert the Bruce.

60. The row of thatched cottages on the right was for estate workers employed by the owners of Braidwood House, which was built in 1820 by Nathaniel Stevenson. The cottages in the foreground were at the main gate of the 'big house'. They remained in a similar condition to the photograph above until the 1960s, when they unfortunately had to be demolished after the thatched roofs caught fire.

61. This is the staff at Braidwood Station. Fruit from the nearby orchards and fields used to be sent every night by refrigerated train to Bradford Market. This station is no longer used.

62. Law Junction was a very important link on the main line south to London. The line was officially opened in 1848, just up the track near Garriongill. All trains going south from Glasgow and Perth to England had to pass through Law. The postal trains from Aberdeen and Glasgow were combined each night at this junction and mail was sorted en route. At the end of the nineteenth century the bustle at this junction would also be caused by the freight traffic from the many small branch lines leading to the local collieries, which sent 2,000 tons daily to the Lanarkshire steel works.

63. The Wilson's and Clyde Coal Company was one of the companies involved in the collieries around Law Village. In the mid-nineteenth century, there were ten collieries around Law and 878 men were employed in coal mining in 1896. This was the boom period, after which mining declined, until in 1948 there were only twelve miners left in Law, none of whom worked locally. This picture shows the aftermath of a fire at a Law colliery when the pit-head machinery was destroyed.

64. The Wilson and Clyde Coal Company laid the foundation for the site of today's Law Village, part of which is shown in this photograph taken around 1905. It shows the bottom of Lawhill Road with the Welfare Hall on the left. This hall was built before 1897 and was originally called The Wilson Public Hall. The company also built houses for its workers. The longest row was Wilson's Row, which had around forty houses in one continuous line. Prior to this building by the Company, Law was at the top of the hill and was called Law of Mauldslie.

65. Most people today probably imagine that missionaries were only sent to far away countries, but church records show that in 1870, missionaries were sent to the village of Law. They were paid for by the Reverend Dr. Wylie, who was minister of Carluke Parish Church at that time. However, it was not the Parish Church which was built first in Law, but the Free Church in Station Road, which opened for worship in 1879. The Parish Church, shown in this photograph, was built soon after. A great deal of information has still to come to light about this interesting picture. It records a visit by the Moderator of The General Assembly of the Church of Scotland and may have been taken when the Free Church united with the Church of Scotland in 1929. The two congregations merged in 1940 and used this church for worship until 1978, when they moved to the church in Station Road. After that, the old parish church lay empty until it was demolished in September 1985.

66. Before the days of labour-saving machines in the home, many women must have had little time for leisure activities. This is one of the rare photographs we have come across which shows women enjoying some time away from their daily routine. These women are having a pleasant day out near Law. Their clothing, especially their footwear, would now be considered totally unsuitable for such a hot summer's day!

67. Walking out on a Sunday was a favourite occupation of Carluke folk in the days when the Sabbath was strictly observed. This is Jacob's Ladder which led down to the Gill near Mauldslie Estate. It is one of the many beautiful rights-of-way in the parish.

68. Carluke Golf Club was instituted in 1893. Fields at Whitehill Farm and Shieldhill Farm were first considered but proved unsuitable and the first permanent site was at Langshaw Farm, which can be see in the background of this photograph. When a five-year lease brought security in 1897, the members decided to erect a clubhouse. This was completed a year later, only to be moved again in 1903 so that running water could be installed. The desire to expand the course to eighteen holes made it necessary for the golf club to look for a new site. After five years of negotiations with Hallcraig Estate, agreement was reached on 1st April 1911 that a golf course could be laid out. Carluke Golf Club still uses this site today, and in 1985 added a large extension to the clubhouse.

69. Carluke Milton Rovers were founded in 1887 and are thus one of the oldest Junior Football teams in Scotland. They formerly played at Kirk Road and Whitehill Park and about 1919 transferred to their present ground at Loch Park on the Lanark Road.

70. Carpet bowling has always been a favourite indoor sport for the winter months. This photograph of the Roadmeetings Club, with the trophies they won in 1925-26, is just one example of the many clubs in the parish. Back row, left to right: Harry Sloan, Chistopher Steele, Geordie Sirrell and Will Paterson. Front: Rob Sirrell, unknown, Jack Tait and Bob Gordon.

71. Carluke Amateur Operatic Society gave its first performance in November 1922 in the Rankin Memorial Hall. HMS Pinafore was a popular choice from the works of Gilbert and Sullivan. The leading man was Clifford Caroll, seated centre. Other parts were taken by Charles Kay, Jessie Hobart, Joan Auld (née Young), David Willocks, James Luck, John Robertson, James Veitch and Miss Dickson. The society celebrated its Diamond Jubilee in 1981 and today performs in the District Hall, Carnwath Road.

72. Carluke had its keen pioneer photographers like any other town around 1906. This is the town camera club taken at the Falls of Clyde on New Year's Day. The boy is believed to be one of the Hinksman family (see photograph 9). The white-bearded gentleman is Mr. Chalmers from Yieldshield.

CARLUKE HORTICULTURAL SOCIETY.—Jubilee Show, 30th August, 1901.

R. S. Brooks, G. Gray, W. Gold, A. Davidson.
C. Harris, R. Chalmers, J. Cockburn, T. Galbraith, J. Shirlaw, W. Sturrock, R. Kerr, R. Morton.
A. Dempster, J. Barclay, J. Brown, T. Grossart, T. Morton, A. Beveridge, T. Gray, A. Stewart, D. Bryson.
Treas. Vice-Pres. Pres. Secy.

73. Horticulture was very important to the industry of Carluke. Fruitgrowing in the orchards on the banks of the Clyde and glasshouses for growing crops, such as Clydeside tomatoes, brought jobs to many. This photograph of the town's Horticultural Society shows that growing flowers for pleasure was also a keen interest.

74. Carluke Bowling Club was formed after a meeting in 1864 in the Useful Knowledge Society's rooms in Kirkton Street. The turf cost £4 per half acre and was procured from Mr. Robert Forrest of the Gair Farm. The green was officially opened by Dr. Selkirk on 31st May 1865. The Ladies Section was inaugurated on 28th May 1930.

75. The other bowling club in the town is called Castlehill Bowling Club but its full name was Castlehill Colliery Bowling Club. The bowling green was built off the Belstane Road near the Dyke Row. The work was done by the miners from the colliery who used hutches from the pit to help cart the earth. Some of the men are shown here. They are, from the back left: Messrs. Megahy, Lenny, McMahon, McKenna, Smith and Baxter. The child is unknown but perhaps a reader may recognise him or herself. The club was officially opened on 11th June 1921 by Mr. Matthew Brown, general manager of the Shotts Iron Company Ltd.

76. When people recall their childhood in a town, they remember not only the buildings but also the people who were important to them. Every town had its 'characters' – men or women who stood out from the ordinary in some way or other – and we felt that our history of the town in pictures would not be complete without mentioning one of them. We have chosen 'Punkie Willie', because even today, local people recall their memories of him with a smile! Willie Ewings lived in a cottage between the chapel and the parish church in Mount Stewart Street. He used to sweep people's chimneys and also acted as town crier. He was often to be seen going about the town ringing a small hand-bell and announcing the latest news!